THE HEY-DAY
of the
GREAT ATLANTIC LINERS

By
Rex Barratt

By the same author:-
> A short History of the Parish and Church of St. George-the-Martyr, Truro.
> Life in Edwardian Truro.
> The Story of the Truro City Bowling Club.
> Stately Homes in and around Truro.
> Memories of a Truronian in War and Peace.

PHOTOGRAPHS:
Grateful acknowledgments to F.E. Gibson, of Scilly; the Cunard Steamship Co., M.E. Thorpe; Stewart Bale Ltd., R.W.R. Squier; H.L. Douch and the Royal Institution of Cornwall; the Post Office; Osborne Studios; and W.G. Thorpe.

The author expresses his thanks to Messrs David & Charles publishers of "The Atlantic Liners 1925 - 1970" by Frederick Emmons, for permission to use data furnished in that book regarding speed records, formation of Steamship Lines, dates of launching and size of some of the trans-Atlantic Liners, particularly those built after the end of the first World War.

ISBN 0 907566 57 X

1983

Published by: Dyllansow Truran - Truran Publications, Trewirgie, Redruth.

Printed by: Helston Printers, 12 Wendron Street, Helston, Cornwall.

ILLUSTRATIONS

Page

INTRODUCTION

The half-century or so preceding the outbreak of the first World War in August, 1914, saw the emigration of thousands of Cornishmen and women. During the sixty years from 1861 to 1921 the population of the county declined by 48,831 - from 369, 390 to 320,559 - over 13%. Some went to South Africa and Australia and New Zealand but the great majority took the sea-journey to the United States of America where their skills, particularly in mining and quarrying, were sure of adequate reward. As a boy living in the State of Rhode Island in the first decade of the twentieth century I well remember the many Cornishmen then employed in the granite quarries and other industries of that State, and it is well known that Cornish immigrants played a large part in developing the iron mines in Minnesota.

This book, which does not by any means claim to be a comprehensive history of the great liners which traversed the Atlantic before the 1914 - 1918 War, may stir the memories of many who can recall those days and be of interest to those of Cornish descent who have often heard their parents or grandparents talk of their sea voyages. I myself had the pleasure of travelling on two of these great ships - the *Carmania* and the *Philadelphia* - an unforgettable experience - and can thus speak from personal knowledge of the excellence of both the accommodation and the cuisine afforded to passengers of those days.

Readers who know Cornwall will be interested in that part of the book headed *The Perilous Sea* and especially to my recording of some of the notable Atlantic liners which came to grief - not a few of them on its rock-bound coasts - in the latter days of the nineteenth century and the early days of the twentieth.

The reason why this book covers only the period to August, 1914, lies in the fact that the outbreak of War then brought the emigrant flow to the Americas to an abrupt halt. Four years of warfare sadly diminished the principal steamship lines and the great pre-war German liners were, in 1918 and 1919, taken over by the victorious Allies. Expectations of a post-war boom were largely quashed by the Dillingham Immigration Act of 1923 by which mass emigration of the United States was severely restricted. As a member of the House of Representatives said - "the melting-pot was to have a rest."

For some years, however, large, luxurious and ever faster steamships continued in service. The *Empress of Britain, Rex, Conte di Savoia, Normandie,* and particularly the *Queen Mary, Queen Elizabeth* and the *United States,* are names which spring to mind. In a few final paragraphs I have made mention of these ships none of which, however, remains on a regular trans-Atlantic run today. All the great Liners were, notwithstanding massive Government subsidies, driven out by charter flights and air travel generally. As a result many ships were adapted to cruising and today the great Atlantic Liners are, like the famous clipper-ships of the previous century, a thing of the past.

Rex Barratt.

THE HEY-DAY OF THE GREAT ATLANTIC LINERS

If these days in which we live may be called 'the age of the airplane,' then the closing decades of the last century and the first of the twentieth might well be known as 'the age of the great ocean liner.' Day after day on all the oceans of the world great steamers carrying thousands of passengers, mails, specie, and cargo, could be seen ploughing their sea-way between continent and continent, and year after year new ships were coming off the stocks in ship-building yards throughout the world. In 1909 for instance some 723 new steamships were launched:-

	Number	Tonnage
In Great Britain & Ireland	452	468,203
In the United States	48	160,201
In Germany	62	121,438
In Holland and Belgium	37	60,502
In Japan	16	45,246
In France	19	43,748
In Norway	45	30,741
In Austria-Hungary	16	22,235
In other countries of the world	28	50,671

By 1910 of the world's total tonnage the proportion owned and sailed under the British flag was 45.36%; under the United States flag 12.6%; and under the German flag 10.34%

While it is true that these great monarchs of the ocean provided world-wide links it was those which crossed and recrossed the Atlantic that attracted the greatest attention. They were the best known of all ocean liners and exhibited the highest standards of comfort - even luxury - for their passengers, and their great size and speed aroused universal interest.

Throughout the nineteenth century and the early days of the twentieth, millions of people in all parts of Europe heard the call of the New World. As word of virgin land which could be acquired cheaply ($1.25 an acre), and of thriving and rapidly expanding industries paying high wages, spread through Europe there was no lack of response to that call. It has been reliably estimated that 35,000,000 immigrants had entered the United States by the close of the 19th century or soon after. Among several causes which led up to this great mass emigration from the Old World were political unrest; oppression; low pay; unemployment; and (as in the case of Ireland) famine and near-starvation. So far as Ireland is concerned the late President Kennedy, whose great-grandfather, Patrick Kennedy, had emigrated in the 1840's, once said: "In the century from 1820 to 1920 four and a half million people left Ireland to come to the United States."

It was not only emigrants, however, who were provided for on these well-appointed ships; the affluent and wealthy on both sides of the Atlantic found in them everything they could desire or want to make the crossing delightful and memorable.

EARLY DAYS

The *Savannah* was the first steamship to cross the Atlantic. A wooden paddle-wheel ship built at New York, 130ft. in length with a gross tonnage of 320, she ran from Savannah to Liverpool in 1819 in twenty-five days, but under steam for only a part of the time, having been built originally as a sailing ship and still relying very largely on sail.

Fourteen years later the *Royal William* made a similar crossing from Quebec, to commemmorate which the Canadian Government issued a special centenary postage stamp in August, 1933.

Steamship "Royal William" depicted crossing the Atlantic from Quebec to Liverpool in 1833.

Although these two ships, assisted largely by sails it is true, had proved that it was feasible for a steamer to cross the Atlantic a speaker at a meeting of the British Association in 1838 was rash enough to say:- "Men might as well project a voyage to the moon as attempt to employ steam across the stormy Atlantic." In that same year his words were proved wrong because before the year had ended crossings of the "stormy Atlantic" were made by the *Sirius* built at Leith, 178ft. in length, 703 tons; by a second *Royal William,"* 145ft. in length, 720 tons, which had been chartered from the City of Dublin Steam Packet Co., and by the *Great Western,* designed by Isambard Kingdom Brunel who had suggested to the Directors of the Great Western Railway Company that they should have a steamer to ply between Bristol and New York. This steamer was 212ft. in length and 1,340 tons, and was built at Bristol. It was the first steamship to be built with the idea of making regular trans-Atlantic voyages.

The 'Sirius' of 703 tons: the first British steamer to cross the Atlantic in 1838

In reporting the vessel's first voyage the "Royal Cornwall Gazette" of 13th July, 1838, said:-

"The 'Great Western' steamship arrived on Sunday last at Bristol from New York in 12 days and a half; a miracle in navigation totally unprecedented. The 'Great Western' performed the voyage out in 14 days and a half."

The same newspaper in its issue of 21st September, 1838, had this further to say:-

"The triumphant success which has attended all the voyages of the 'Great Western' steamship has given a confirmed stimulus to such undertakings. So great are the advantages of the proprietors in being the only parties in the field with a vessel of sufficient magnitude for profitable voyages between England and New York that their gain will probably be £100,000 in the first year."

Brunell then designed the much larger *Great Britain* also built at Bristol, 274ft. in length, 3,270 tons, the first large ship to use the screw propeller, which made her first voyage from Liverpool to New York in August, 1845, but a year later ran aground on the coast of Ireland. She was subsequently refloated and used in the Australian trade for some time. It was on this steamer that the first England Cricket Team ever to visit Australia travelled in 1861. All the players are said to have worn deer-stalker caps adorned with blue ribbons!

I.K. Brunel's "GREAT BRITAIN" 3,270 tons shortly after launching in 1845. The first large steamship to use the screw propeller. This picture is reproduced by kind permission of the South West Postal Region and is a reproduction of S.W. Postal Region Postcard 15 (b) which is on sale at most Post Office Philatelic counters.

I.K. Brunel's "Great Eastern" - 18,915 tons - launched 1858.

In 1852 Brunel worked out a scheme for a really great ship, the construction of which was begun at Millwall. After several unsuccessful attempts this huge vessel - the *Great Eastern* - was eventually launched in 1858 but did not start her first voyage until September, 1859, by which time Brunel, worn out by worry and overwork, was dying. This enormous ship was 860ft. in length, of 82ft. beam, and 18,915 tons; driven by screw, paddles and sails. On her trial trip what was described as a "terrible explosion" occurred in the ships boiler-room. It was somewhat dramatically described by George Augustus Sala in the 'Daily Telegraph' of 12th September, 1859:-

"Suddenly the reverberation of a tremendous explosion was heard. Then came a crash, then a sweeping, rolling, rumbling sound as of cannon-balls scudding around on the deck below. My next neighbour cried out, "The boiler has burst." On gaining the deck I could at first see nothing but billows of steam rolling towards us."

Actually four men were killed by this explosion and Sala continues:

"One by one, some on the shoulders and in the arms of their comrades, or in one or two cases staggering past, came the unfortunate men who had been scalded in the stoke-hold."

The *Great Eastern* remained the largest steamship then afloat until the White Star Liner *Celtic* was built 43 years later. In 1864 she was chartered for cable-laying and sold for scrap in 1888.

James Bodell (1831-1892) in his Reminiscences gives an account of his trans-Atlantic crossing in 1883 from New York to Liverpool by the Queen Liner *Alaska* described as a steamer of 5,500 tons in which in July of that year he, with 800 other passengers, made the crossing to Queenstown in 6 days 20 hours. This was considered to be a good passage because it was not until 1889 that the Atlantic was crossed by a steamship in less than six days. He was probably referring to the single-screw steamer *Alaska* of 7,142 tons, 500 ft. in length and 50 ft. beam, belonging to the Guion Line, built in Glasgow in 1881.

("A Soldier's View of Empire" - ed. Keith Sinclair - published by The Bodley Head, 1982.)

Meanwhile a pioneer in Atlantic travel had arrived in England. He was Samuel Cunard, a merchant and shipowner, born in Halifax, Nova Scotia, in 1786, who came to Liverpool in 1838 and a year later with George Burns of Glasgow and David MacIver of Liverpool, founded the British & North American Royal Mail Packet Co., which eventually became the Cunard Line. On 4th July, 1840, the first Cunarder, the *Britannia*, started her voyage to Boston with 63 passengers, taking 14 days en route. The *America*, 1,825 tons; the *Asia*, 2,227 tons; and the *Persia*, 3,300 tons, followed; the latter being iron built.

It was on the *Britannia*, 1,150 tons, that Charles Dickens embarked on his first tour of the United States in 1842. Of that ship and its accommodations he subsequently had much to say. What the Cunard advertisements had described as a salon of infinite perspective was, according to Dickens, a narrow apartment not unlike a gigantic hearse with windows. His cabin, he later wrote, was a thoroughly hopeless, preposterous box, and as to the sleeping bunks, "nothing smaller for sleeping in was ever made except coffins."

Cunard paddle-wheeler "Persia" of 3,670 tons.

Improved standards, however, were to come and as steamships grew in size, so living conditions on board improved beyond measure. Cunard formed the idea of a regular service and entered into a contract with the Government for the conveyance of mails. The first Cunard screw steamer for the mail service was the *China* of some 2,539 tons, with an average speed of 13.9 knots, which came into service in 1862.

> *"Sail on! Sail on! ye stately ships*
> *And with your floating bridge the western ocean span."*

THE BEGINNING OF THE HEY-DAY

Over the years constant improvement has been the watchword both of the ship-owner and the ship-builder; the introduction of the iron screw for propulsion in place of side-paddles; the compound engine; the triple expansion and quadruple expansion engines; the turbine (invented by Sir Charles Parsons, O.M. - b. 1854 - d. 1931); better passenger accommodation; improved state-rooms; the sub-division of hulls and the introduction of water-tight bulkheads.

By the first decade of the 20th century the number of steamships crossing the Atlantic had increased beyond measure. Steamers flying the British, American, German, French, Dutch, Italian, Austrian and Spanish ensigns were maintaining fast and regular services between many European ports and those of North and South America. In the days immediately preceding the first World War this trans-Atlantic service was at its height with ever more powerful, larger and faster steamships catering for the needs of emigrants and travellers in general.

As to speed, the *Campania* and *Lucania,* sister ships built in 1893 for the Cunard Steamship Co., by Fairfield Shipbuilding Co., held the record for fast passages across the Atlantic for some years. With twin screws and triple expansion engines they attained speeds of 22 knots. In 1897 the German *'Kaiser Wilhelm der Grosse'* surpassed that record and for some ten years the fastest vessels were those in German ownership. The *'Kaiser Wilhelm II'* raised the record to 23.71 knots. In 1903 the British Government came to an agreement with the Cunard Co., under which the latter were to provide two vessels of a speed of 24 knots for the Royal Mail and passenger service; the ships to be available to the Admiralty in time of War. Subsequently two great ships - the *Mauretania* of 31,938 tons, and the *Lusitania* of 31,550 tons, each driven by Parsons Turbines of 70,000 h.p. and fitted with four screws, were ordered.

The *Lusitania* was the first in service in 1907 and at once regained the Blue-ribband for Britain. The *Lusitania's* 25.85 knots was only beaten by the *Mauretania's* 26.06 knots.

Cunard R.M.S. "Campania" - 12,950 tons.

Cunard R.M.S. "Mauretania" - 31,938 tons.

EVER INCREASING SERVICES

Competition between the numerous companies on the North Atlantic run inevitably became acute and it is not surprising to find that 'mergers' were brought about. In 1901 a group of American capitalists acquired the American, Red Star and Inman Lines. Headed by J. Pierpont Morgan they later acquired the Leyland Line, the White Star Line and the Atlantic Transport Company. In September, 1902, the combination was incorporated in New Jersey as "The International Mercantile Marine Company" with a capital of $12,000,000, and at that time, or soon after, it controlled about one million tons of shipping.

Regarding the type of accommodation the traveller could expect to find on these great steamers, the following extracts from a handbook entitled "FACTS FOR TRAVELLERS" issued to passengers on ships of the International Mercantile Marine Co., in 1909, will indicate, viz:-

"On the deck below the promenade is the dining-saloon whose spacious proportions can accommodate 366 passengers, the ship's entire complement of first-class passengers, with seats at one time. The apartment is situated where there is the least motion - amidships between the two funnels - and is lighted from above by a huge panelled dome of glass, artful in its curving proportions and color treatment, and extending the full length of the saloon. This dome, which has attracted universal admiration, extends to a height of twenty feet, with an arch span of fifty-three feet. At the sides of the room, in place of the usual contracted port-holes, are large rectangular windows assuring perfect ventilation. Small tables in place of the long ones so often found on trans-Atlantic steamers, have made the saloon unusually cozy in appearance.

The key-note of the decorative scheme throughout the ship is brilliance, and the light has been preserved by avoiding dark colors. The whole tone of the dining saloon is one of refinement. The wood employed is white mahogany, and the panels supporting the enormous glass dome represent sea-nymphs disposed in attitudes of playful sports of the sea. Two strikingly beautiful works of sculpture by the famous artist, Karl Bitter, adorn the ends of the saloon and are placed in the arched spaces under the glass dome. In the after space is a figure of Neptune grasping his trident in an attitude of supremacy over the tumultuous waves among which he is seated. At the forward end is a spirited scene, the principal figure of which is a graceful mermaid whose out-stretched arms sustain the gallery of the saloon and above which are to be seen the gilded pipes of the great organ.

Directly forward of the dining-saloon opens the main companionway, a handsome double staircase with treads of easy ascent, from which the library is reached, a magnificent room finished in oak, said to be the largest apartment ever devoted to library purposes on a trans-Atlantic steamer. The book-shelves contain over one thousand choice works of literature which are available to passengers at all times."

These comments apply to the American Line steamers *St. Louis* and *St. Paul* which were said to be the fastest and finest trans-Atlantic steamers ever turned out of an American Shipyard; that of Wm. Cramp & Sons Ship & Engine Building Company of Philadelphia.

Of two other ships of the American Line, the *New York* and the *Philadelphia*, the handbook had this to say:-

"Externally the *New York* and the *Philadelphia* are two of the most beautiful steamships afloat. Their lines are those of a yacht, with graceful bow-sprited stem and long overhang stern. Each has three masts and two funnels.

The grandest feature of these ships is, beyond all doubt,

American Line U.S.M.S. "St. Louis" - 11,629 tons.

U.S.M.S. Philadelphia - 10,433 tons

the first-class dining saloon which is located on the saloon deck. It is a room of noble proportions and extends almost entirely across the ship. Unlike on most steamers, the dining saloon is carried to an immense height, through two decks and a half, and is surmounted by a cathedral glass dome of magnificent design and equisite coloring. The full height is twenty feet, while the length of the arched roof is fifty-three feet, with a span of twenty-five feet. In this grand saloon there are dining places arranged for 271 passengers. At one end of the saloon, and under the gabled archway formed by the domed ceiling, is the grand organ loft, which is accessible also from the promenade deck. A beautiful oriel window occupies the other end communicating with the ladies' drawing room. The small tables in the center of the saloon, seating but a few passengers at each, are disposed longitudinally with the length of the ship, and the revolving arm-chairs are beautifully upholstered and most comfortable. Cozy little alcoves are arranged around the sides of the saloon fitted with small athwartship tables for those who seek home-like privacy.

Well-known artists have collaborated to decorate the saloon in a most charming manner. A white composition of peculiar ductility was used to garnish the woodwork of the arch and organ loft and the paneling is gorgeously embellished by representations of dolphins, sea-nymphs, and tritons, in graceful postures. A large clock is embedded in the front of the gallery, while a huge gilt lyre surmounts the encasement of the organ.

The drawing-room is a perfect gem, adorned and appointed with exquisite taste, and is a favorite haunt of the lady passengers in both fair weather and foul. The white paneled walls and ceiling, striped with gold, give light and brilliance to this apartment. Plate-glass mirrors adorn the side walls; and the furniture of polished mahogany and red upholstery harmonizes perfectly with the polished oak floor and its oriental coverings. An upright grand piano completes the apartment as a social center, and pleasant musicales are often held here.

The smoking-room, very handsomely and comfortably appointed, its dimensions being 45 feet long by 27 feet wide, is the retreat of men who delight in the pleasures of tobacco."

Of what was then described as "the new mammoth steamer *Adriatic*" of the White Star Line, the book had this to say:-

"The march of human progress is at quick step in these twentieth century times, and the building of the White Star Line's new steamship *Adriatic* marked another giant stride toward the acme of steamship construction. From the advent of the White Star Line into the Atlantic trade in 1869, when the first *Oceanic* - now but a pleasant memory of those early days of ocean navigation - reigned empress of the high seas, to the moment when this leviathan *Adriatic* sailed proudly down the Mersey to the ocean completes an epoch of marine achievement never before equaled. The crowning glory of the *Adriatic,* of course, is found in the passenger accommodations which are of the most luxurious type. In the grand saloon of the first class the decorations are most striking and artistic and the appointments harmonious in design. The apartment is paneled in the stately fashion of the period of Charles the Second, and at the same time is painted chastely and simply in a delicate ivory white. A beautiful dome lends its splendour to the dining saloon, the glass being of the palest yellow: and under this translucent canopy are exquisite paintings of beautiful spots in Switzerland, Italy, the Rhine, and the Yellowstone, reminding the traveller of the splendours of nature both at home and abroad.

The string orchestra, as on the other steamers of the White Star Line, assists materially in passing many pleasant hours on board. The orchestra plays both on deck and in the main companionway and possesses a very extensive repertoire.

The *Adriatic* boasts of one of the most magnificent dining-saloons on any Atlantic steamer. The seating arrangements are in the popular 'restaurant' style - small tables studded about the room - an attractive feature contributing much to the pleasure of the passengers. The first-class smoking-room is located on the popular boat-deck and here centers the masculine interest. Cozy comfort is the keynote and the walls hung with stamped leather adorned with pictures of some stirring episodes in English Naval History often echo the hum of conversation and the hearty laughter of good fellowship.

The first-class lounge, a general gathering place for both women and men, will be especially a magnet for social intercourse during the evenings and wet weather. The reading and writing room of the ship, a beautiful apartment, is also accorded a place on the airy boat deck, where it is easily accessible, being most spacious and ornate in its furnishings; and through the windows, which are as large as in an ordinary house, passengers may look out, not upon some stretch of lawn as the room itself might lead one to suspect, but on the tumbling billows of the sea. Here, however, we may stretch our limbs before the home-like fireside, or read our books in a quiet corner. Upon the walls decorated with delicate ornaments in low relief, airy, dainty paintings like those our great-grandmothers used to love, stand in their panels, and over all comes the subdued yet efficient light of the shaded electrics. Here, too, the desks and stationery invite one to correspondence.

A large number of suites of apartments - each separate and complete in all appointments - is provided, each consisting of bedroom, sitting room, bathroom etc: affording the highest type of luxurious style - the last word in the matter of bodily comfort. On the upper and lower promenade decks are located also a number of the large staterooms which form such an important feature and are so much sought after in the first class accommodations of the *Baltic, Cedric, Celtic,* and *Arabic;* and the single berth rooms, so popular with the traveling public, are also to be found here - comfortable in every detail.

An electric elevator in the first-class from the saloon deck to the upper promenade has proved a pleasant and useful innovation; and the Information Bureau is a source of satisfaction to the passengers.

A dark-room has been fitted for the use of those who enjoy photography and no doubt it will continue to be well patronized.

The turkish bath, however, is one of the most novel of the many innovations on this immense steamer. Here are all the most modern accessories for the bath with a corps of expert attendants. The novel electric light baths have their devotees and the fullest benefits of the sea-voyage with its salt water baths can be had aboard. With the accompanying gymnasium and the wide expanse of four promenade decks, the *Adriatic* takes first place in the important matter of opportunities for exercise and recreation."

Whilst this fulsome praise was lavished on the first-class accommodation, much less space was taken to describe that for the second and third-class passengers. On the *Adriatic* -

"Immediately abaft the first-class staterooms are the accommodations for passengers in the second-class; a comfortable and beautiful dining-saloon with 240 seats, the room being done in white and gold, with mahogany furniture

White Star Line S.S. Adriatic

First Class Saloon, S.S. Adriatic

upholstered in dainty moquette. The ladies' room is a gracefully planned apartment furnished in satinwood with inlaid panels, the furniture here being also in substantial mahogany, The general lounge has handsome oak furniture, easy tub chairs and all the coziness such a room requires. The staterooms in second-class are decorated in white paneling, the berths being of comfortable size and design.

The third-class passengers are located in the section aft and, to a limited extent, forward, a very acceptable feature being the two, three and four-berth rooms in large numbers provided for married couples and families. The commodious and cleanly dining-rooms, fitted with tables and revolving chairs, add their attractions to other features provided for passengers in third-class."

NOTABLE TRANS-ATLANTIC STEAMERS pre-1914

AMERICAN LINE	Tonnage	Length - ft.	Beam - ft.
St. Louis	11,629	554	63
St. Paul	11,269	554	63
New York	10,799	576	63
Philadelphia	10,433	576	63
Haverford	11,635	547	59
Merion	11,621	547	59
Friesland	6,409	470	51
Westernland	5,708	455	47
Noordland	5,150	416	47

Inman Liner "City of Rome" - 8,144 tons. One of the most graceful steamships ever to cross the Atlantic.

Dining Saloon, S.S. Friesland.

The American Line was founded at Philadelphia in 1871, with the Red Star Line, under the corporate name "International Navigation Company," and in 1886 they purchased the famous Inman Line which had maintained regular sailings between New York and Liverpool since 1856 with the 'City of Paris,' 10,670 tons; the 'City of Rome,' 8,144 tons; 'City of Berlin,' 5,481 tons: 'City of Richmond,' 4,623 tons: and 'City of Brussells,' 3,081 tons. This company's steamers had been the first which regularly undertook the conveyance of third-class passengers and in 1869 the 'City of Brussels' made the eastbound crossing in 7 days 22 hours which at that time was a record. During the Spanish-American War in 1898 four steamships of the American Line were commissioned by the U.S. Navy, the *St. Paul* being put under the command of Capt. Sigsbee whose own battleship - the *Maine* - had been blown up at Havana on 15th February, 1898.

It was on a steamer of the American Line - U.S.M.S. *Philadelphia* - that Guglielmo Marconi made several Atlantic crossings in 1902 in order to prove that wireless signals could be transmitted thousands of miles around the curvature of the earth. The steamship had its masts heightened so that the ship's aerial was 150ft. above the deck.

ATLANTIC TRANSPORT LINE	Tonnage	Length-ft.	Beam-ft.
Minnewaska	14,220	616	66
Minnehaha	13,403	616	66
Minneapolis	13,401	616	66
Minnetonka	13,398	616	66
Mesaba	6,833	495	52

Atlantic Transport Co's. "Minnetonka" - 13.398 tons.

Dining Saloon
on board the
"Minnetonka."

27

The Atlantic Transport Line's inception in 1885 at Baltimore led to the inauguration in 1892 of a popular service from New York to London with the entire passenger accommodation of the steamers devoted to "First-class passengers only."

DOMINION LINE	Tonnage	Length-ft.	Beam-ft.
Canada	9,413	514	58
Kensington	8,669	495	57
Southwark	8,607	495	57
Dominion	6,618	456	50
Vancouver	5,292	448	45
Ottawa	5,071	448	45

The Dominion Line began business as The Liverpool & Mississippi Steamship Co., in 1870; subsequently changed to the Mississippi & Dominion Steamship Co., and, again, to the Dominion Line. It held a commanding position in Canadian shipping, making use of the St. Lawrence River in summer and using Portland as the western terminus in winter.

Dominion Liner "Canada" - 9,413 tons

LEYLAND LINE	Tonnage	Length-ft.	Beam-ft.
Devonian	10,418	571	59
Winifredian	10,405	571	59
Canadian	9,301	549	59
Cestrian	8,823	529	59
Bohemian	8,548	529	59

The Leyland Line - Frederick Leyland & Co Ltd., - began a passenger service between Liverpool and Boston in 1895 with the sister ships *Victorian* and *Armenian.* The steamers of this line provided accommodation for first-class passengers only.

Leyland Liner S.S. "Devonian" - 10,418 tons.

RED STAR LINE	Tonnage	Length-ft.	Beam-ft.
Lapland	17,000	600	70
Finland	12,760	578	60
Kroonland	12,760	578	60
Vaderland	12,018	580	60
Zeeland	11,905	580	60
Samland	9,710	506	58
Gothland	7,669	504	53
Marquette	7,057	502	52
Menominee	6,919	490	52
Manitou	6,849	490	52

The Red Star Line was orginally a Belgian Company formed by the Societe Anoyme de Navigation Belge-Americaine. The first sailing was by an iron screw steamer (*Vaderland*) in January 1873, under the Belgian flag, from Antwerp to Philadelphia. The *Samland* and *Gothland* carried third-class passengers only.

Red Star Liner "Kroonland." 12,760 tons.

WHITE STAR LINE	Tonnage		Tonnage
Olympic	46,439	Titanic	46,329
Adriatic	24,541	Baltic	23,876
Cedric	21,035	Celtic	20,904
Oceanic	17,274	Arabic	15,801
Laurentic	14,000	Republic	15,378
Megantic	14,000	Cretic	13,518
Romanic	11,394	Canopic	12,097
Teutonic	10,000	Majestic	10,000
*Britannic	48,158		

*The *Britannic* was built in 1914-15 and never saw service as a passenger liner but was fitted out as a hospital ship for the transport of wounded troops. On 1st Nov. 1916, she struck a mine whilst bound from Naples to Mudros and sank with the loss of 28 lives.

The White Star Line was founded in 1867 by Thomas Ismay. The company's first steamer - *Oceanic* 3,708 tons - left Liverpool bound for New York in March, 1871. and within a year had been joined by five other steamers all built by Harland & Wolff at Belfast. The depression of the 1930's saw the Line merged with the Cunard Steamship Co., in 1934.

After the sinking of the *Titanic* in 1912 her sister ship, the *Olympic*, underwent a considerable amount of reconstruction at the ship-yard of Harland & Wolff; had her bulkheads raised; was made capable of keeping afloat even if six of her water-tight compartments were flooded; and had several more Lifeboats added to her existing complement. She then remained in service until the outbreak of the first World War when she became a troopship. Whilst so employed in May, 1918, she rammed and sank a German submarine and, in

White Star Line S.S. Oceanic

White Star Line S.S. Baltic

1919, on resuming normal service, became one of the first Atlantic Liners to become oil-fired. In 1934, in thick fog, the *Olympic* was in collision with the Nantucket Lightship off the coast of Massachusetts and in the following year was sold for scrap and broken up.

White Star Liner "Britannic," 48,158 in use as a Hospital Ship in 1916.

CUNARD LINE

	Tonnage		Tonnage
Mauretania	31,938	Lusitania	31,550
Caronia	19,687	Carmania	19,525
Saxonia	14,067	Ivernia	14,067
Lucania	14,067	Campania	12,952
Umbria	8,120	Etruria	8,120
*Aquitania	45,647		

*After only three crossings crossings in the summer of 1914 became a Hospital Ship and then a Troopship - 1915 - 1919.

The Cunard Steamship Co. Ltd., can probably claim to be the oldest and most famous on the North Atlantic. Following its inception in 1839, as previously related, it entered on a period of great prosperity. In 1906-07 the construction of the *Lusitania* and the *Mauretania* was begun to augment the eight ships then in the regular Europe-America service. During the 1914-1918 War nine Cunarders were lost by enemy action including the *Lusitania* torpedoed off the coast of Ireland with the loss of over 1,100 lives. Today the Cunard Line operate what is probably the most famous passenger ship afloat - the *Queen Elizabeth 2.*

During the Boer War (1899 - 1902) the Cunarder *Umbria,* the White Star *Majestic*, and the former Inman Liner *City of Rome* were used as troopships to carry troops from England to Cape Town; the last named being scrapped shortly afterwards.

ALLAN LINE

	Tonnage		Tonnage
Tunisian	10,576	Victorian	10,685
Virginian	10,687	Calgarian	18,000
Alsatian	18,481	Scotian	10,491

An artist's impression of the sinking of the Cunard liner "Lusitania" after being struck by a torpedo from a German submarine 7th May, 1915, off the coast of Ireland.

Cunard R.M.S. Carmania - 19,525 tons - first Cunarder to be propelled by turbines (1904). As an armed merchant cruiser, engaged and sank the German armed liner Cap Trafalgar (18,700 tons) on 14th September, 1914.

The *Victorian* and the *Virginian* are said to be the first trans-Atlantic Liners propelled by turbines.

At the conclusion of the Peninsular War, Capt. Alexander Allan began a service between the Clyde and Canada. In 1852 a tender submitted by Sir Hugh Allan, one of Alexander Allan's sons, for a weekly mail service to Canada was accepted by the Canadian Government and the Allan Line of steamers came into existence. In 1917 the company was taken over by the Canadian Pacific Steamship Co.

ANCHOR LINE

Transylvania	Caledonia	Cameronia ... ...
Columbia	California	Tuscania ... ...

The Anchor Line was a Scottish Steamship Company founded in 1852 to provide shipping for the North American trade. Its first steamer - the *Tempest* - sailed on 11th October, 1856. The *Columbia* was the sole survivor of the six Atlantic Liners being operated by this Company in 1914, by which time it had been acquired by the Cunard.

CANADIA PACIFIC	Tonnage		Tonnage
Express of Britain	15,646	Empress of Ireland	15,646

Canadian-Pacific Liner "EMPRESS OF BRITAIN" - 42,450 tons - (The second of that name: launched 1931: lost by enemy action 1940)

This Company, in 1903, purchased the Canadian interests of Elder, Demster & Co., including some 15 ships which were providing an emigrant service from Europe to Quebec and Montreal (summer) and to St. John, N.B., (winter). In 1917 the Company took over the Allan Line and subsequently renamed the *Tunisian* as the *Marburn*, the *Victorian* as the *Marloch,* the *Alsatian* as the *Empress of France,* and the *Scotian* as the *Marglen.* During the 1914 - 1918 War the *Scotian* (which had previously been the *Statendam* of the Holland-Amerika Line) was used as a Troopship.

Mention may be made of another steamship of the Canadian Pacific Line namely the s.s. *Montrose* of 5,341 tons plying between Antwerp and Quebec. Originally a cargo vessel she had been adapted to carry a small number of cabin passengers and a large number of emigrants as steerage passengers. It was on this steamer that Hawley Harvey Crippen and Ethel LeNeve travelled in July, 1910, after the murder of Crippen's wife. The story of how they were overtaken and arrested by Chief Inspector Dew of Scotland Yard who followed them on the much faster White Star Liner *Laurentic* was the sensation of the day. The *Montrose* ended her career in 1914 when she foundered on the Goodwin Sands.

DONALDSON LINE

Athenia	Letitia ... ...
Saturnia	Cassandra ... ...

The Donaldson Line was established at Glasgow in 1855 originally to provide a service to and from South America but transferred its operations to Canada in 1876 as the result of heavy emigration, and a regular service from Glasgow to St. John, N.B., Quebec and Montreal, was begun at the close of the 19th century. Shortly after the outbreak of the second World War the Donaldson Liner *Athenia* was the first passenger ship to be sunk by a German submarine - on 4th September, 1939.

UNDER FOREIGN FLAGS

GERMAN. The Hamburg-American Line had been founded in 1847 to operate a fleet between Hamburg and New York. Its first screw steamer was the *Borussia* which left Hamburg on 1st July, 1856, and a few weeks later the *Hammonia* came into service. At that time there were considerable numbers of Germans desirous of emigrating and the company was assured of many passengers. By 1861 there were two sailings each week and by 1914 the Hamburg-American Line could claim to be the largest trans-Atlantic ship owning company of them all. It had absorbed the old Atlas Line; the Hansc Line; the Rickmers Line, and, in conjunction with the Norddeutscher Lloyd, the

Hamburg-Amerika Liner "Deutschland" - 14500 tons.

Hamburg-Amerika Liner "Kaiserin Auguste Victoria." 24,581 tons.

Kinsing Line; and had steamers running between Hamburg and New York, Portland, Baltimore, Boston, Philadelphia, Galveston, New Orleans and Canadian ports. It was also maintaining services from Stettin to Central and South American ports; to the West Indies and to China and Japan. The Chairman of this Company for many years was Albert Ballin who, although a Jew, became a close personal friend of Kaiser Wilhelm II who, with his suite which included 9 Admirals, took a Spring cruise in 1905 in the liner *Hamburg* to the Mediterranean and North Africa where he landed at Tangier and made one of his notorious speeches implying that he would support the Sultan of Morocco to resist any French attempts to control that country.

One of the finest ships built with emigrants particularly in view was probably the *Cleveland* of this Line, 587 ft. in length, of 65 ft. beam, and of 17,000 tons, capable of a speed of 16 knots, which could accommodate no less than 3,200 passengers and a crew of 360.

The *Deutschland* of 14,500 tons, was the first Atlantic Liner of exceed a speed of 23 knots at sea. Other large pre-1914 steamers of this line were: *Blucher* 12,350 tons; *Kaiserin Augusta Victoria* 24,581 tons; *Amerika* 22,622 tons; and the *Imperator* and *Vaterland* both of over 50,000 tons. When War broke out in August, 1914, the *Bismarck* was nearing completion and at the conclusion of hostilities was taken over by the Allies and became the White Star Liner *Majestic* 56,551 tons; while the *Imperator* became the Cunard Liner *Berengaria*.

It was on the *Berengaria* that the Prince of Wales travelled as a private passenger from Southampton to New York on his visit to the United States in August, 1924.

The Norddeutscher Lloyd Line was founded in 1856 by H.H. Meir and orders were given for the construction of four iron screw steamers. The first voyage was that of the *Bremen* in June, 1858. Other notable steamers of this line were the *Goeben,* 8,800 tons, and the *Scharnhorst* 8,287 tons (1904 - 1906). The *Kaiser Wilhelm der Grosse,* 14,350 tons, as previously mentioned, made the westbound crossing on her maiden voyage in 1897 at an average speed of 21.39 knots, thus becoming the fastest and one of the largest ships then afloat. This line also operated and owned the *Kronzprinz Wilhelm,* 14,908 tons; *Kaiser Wilhelm II,* 19,361 tons; *Kronprinzessin Cecilie,* 19,503 tons; and the *George Washington,* 25,507 tons. The last-named was interned at New York in 1914, subsequently used by the United States as a troopship and was the steamer which conveyed President Wilson to attend the Versailles Peace Conference in 1919.

It is estimated that the steamers of the Norddeutscher Lloyd line carried nearly a quarter of a million passengers across the Atlantic in the year 1913, which gives some indication of the scale of emigration from Central Europe at that time.

FRENCH. The Compagnie Generale Transatlantique was incorporated in 1861 and its first steamer, the paddle-wheel *Washington,* left Le Havre for New York in 1864. In the same year the Company acquired the paddle-wheel steamer *Napoleon III* built at Greenock. In 1881 a new fleet was begun for the Atlantic service with the construction of the single-screw steamer *La Normandie* at Barrow-in-Furness. Ten years later the twin-screw steamers *La Touraine* and *L'Aquitane* came into service. A mail contract was arranged in 1898 with the following steamships in service:

France	...	...	... 23,666 tons:	*La Provence*	...	... 13,753 tons:
Rochambeau	...	... 12,678 tons:	*La Savoie*	...	... 11,168 tons:
Chicago	...	...	... 9,350 tons:			

Cyprien Fabre et Cie, of Marseilles, began operating a Marseilles - New York service in 1874. By 1914 it had seven steamers under its flag including the *Venezia - Sant' Anna - Canada* - and the 3-funnelled *Patria* of 11,885 tons.

DUTCH. The Holland-Amerika Line running between Rotterdam and New York recorded its first sailing in 1872 by the small 1,700 ton steamship *Rotterdam.* In 1914 this company had four well-found and well-known steamships on the Atlantic run:

Rotterdam	...	... 24,149 tons:	*Noordam*	...	... 12,538 tons:
Nieu Amsterdam	... 17,149 tons:	*Rijndam*	...	...	... 12,535 tons:

They were all built by Harland & Wolff at Belfast between 1901 and 1908.

It was on the *Rotterdam* that the German Military Attache, Franz von Papen, travelled back from New York early in 1916 when he had been declared persona non grata by the U.S. Government. I well remember this steamer calling at Falmouth en route to Rotterdam with him aboard. He was, of course, afforded diplomatic safe conduct, Holland then being neutral.

This was the man who subsequently became the last Chancellor of Germany in 1923 before Hitler seized power. During the second World-War he was the German Ambassador to Turkey and was tried at Nuremberg in 1946 but was acquitted.

It must not be taken that this is a complete list of all the passenger steamers plying between Europe and America in the years before the 1914-1918 War. At that time steamships were also crossing the Atlantic from Swedish Danish, Norwegian, Italian, Russian, Austrian and Spanish ports.

*Not to be confused with another liner of that name launched in 1958.

THE PERILOUS SEA

Despite the marvellous skill exhibed by designers, ship-builders, master-mariners and crews, it was inevitable that the sea and, in some cases, the rock-bound coasts of Cornwall where "sea-fogs pitch their tents and mists from the mighty Atlantic" should take their toll of these great ships. It is quite understandable why the hymn containing the words "O hear us when we cry to Thee for those in peril on the sea" was so frequently sung in Cornish churches and chapels.

Instances of trans-Atlantic steamships being lost by fire and explosion are rare. One such was that of the Royal Mail Steam Packet Co's *Amazon* of 2,250 tons and 300 ft. in length, described as being "a splendid vessel," which sank about 110 miles south-west of Scilly on 2nd January, 1852, with the loss of 161 lives. This newly-built two funnelled ship, driven by paddles and sails, was outward bound from Southampton to the West Indies and the Gulf of Mexico and in heading down the English Channel had experienced strong head winds. With a crew of over 120 and some 70 odd passengers, general cargo, mails, and a stock of explosives, she was going at full speed when a fire broke out suddenly forward on the starboard side. The flames are said to have "rushed up the gangway which is in front of the foremost funnei," then quickly spread to the stacks of coal which were being carried, to trussess of hay on deck, enveloping the ship which was constructed of pine fir with great rapidity. The fire was followed by a terrific explosion and the *Amazon* disappeared beneath the waves. Three of the steamers Lifeboats managed to get away safely with 58 survivors who were picked up by other ships within a few days. One boat, however, with 13 survivors drifted well out into the Bay of Biscay before rescue.

Seven of the ship's complement, all of whom, except midshipman Vincent, were drowned, were Cornishmen, viz: - the Captain William Symons, Falmouth; 2nd officer C.H. Treweeke, Falmouth: 4th officer G.H. Goodbridge, Falmouth; Midshipman W. Vincent, Falmouth; Able seamen W. Fox, Falmouth; C. Leddra, St. Ives; and William Stone, Ludgvan. ("Royal Cornwall Gazette" - 16th January 1852).

Another early trans-Atlantic liner to meet disaster was the *Arctic,* 2,860 tons, of the Collins Line which sank in dense fog off the coast of Newfoundland in 1854, after being in collision with a French steamer, with the loss of 346 lives. Two years later the *Pacific,* a sister ship of the *Arctic,* and the first to cross the Atlantic in 9 days, whilst on a voyage from Liverpool to New York was sunk without trace; very probably after running into an iceberg. The Collins Line was an American Company which had been founded by Edward K. Collins in 1846, and, with the help of a subsidy from the U.S. Congress, had begun trans-Atlantic sailings with four very fine steamers all of which were said to have been considerably better furnished and fitted out than the then current Cunarders. Its attempt to challenge the latter, however, was a failure and on Congress withdrawing the subsidy in 1858 the line collapsed. Collins' wife and two children were drowned in the wreck of the *Arctic.*

The Inman Line *City of Boston* left Halifax for Liverpool on 28th January, 1870, with 177 on board. Nothing more was ever heard of her.

In his Diaries (extracts from which have recently been published) the Rev. Francis Kilvert - 1840-1879 - makes reference under date "Tuesday December morrow 1873" to the sinking of what he somewhat quaintly describes as the largest and finest steamship that ever swam beside the *Great Eastern.* He was referring, of course, to the sinking of the splendidly equipped French liner *Ville du Havre,* of 5,000 tons, belonging to the Transatlantique Steamship Company, with the loss of 226 lives in mid-Atlantic after being in collision with the Clyde clipper-ship *Loch Earn* of Glasgow, on 21st November, 1873. With 135 passengers, 6 stowaways and a crew of 172, the *Ville du Havre* was homeward bound from New York to Havre when in a heavy sea the force of the collision ripped open the steamer's iron plates and she sank within some fifteen minutes. The *Loch Earn* picked up 87 survivors who were subsequently transferred to the American ship *Tremountain* and brought safely to Cardiff. ("R.C. Gazette," 27th Nov. 1873.)

The White Star liner *Atlantic* ran aground on the coast of Nova Scotia in 1873 with the loss of nearly 600 lives and, at about the same time, the *City of New York* of the Inman Line, became a total loss after grounding outside Queenstown Harbour in Ireland.

On 7th May, 1875, one of the largest steamships of that day, the German s.s. *Schiller* on passage from New York to Hamburg via Plymouth, struck the Retarrier Ledges - a reef off the Scillies - and foundered with the loss of 310 lives. It was reported that a strong wind was blowing and there was thick fog. The navigating officers apparently had no idea that the ship was so close in to the land. After striking, the *Schiller* held together for some time but only 44 of the passengers and crew, some of whom had climbed into the rigging, survived. Bodies continued to be washed up on the beaches of the Islands for several days and 40 were buried in a mass-grave at Old Town Churchyard on one day. The 'Royal Cornwall Gazette' of the 15th May, 1875, devoted the best part of two whole pages to an account of this wreck of which the following are extracts:-

> "Awful Catastrophe at Scilly. Loss of 310 lives with mails and bullion. The most serious and fatal shipwreck that has occurred for many a long year occurred at Scilly on Friday night. The whole coast of Great Britain has known no such awful catastrophe since the wreck of the *Royal Charter.* In the whole magnificent fleet of the Eagle Line running between Hamburg

"Majestic" (ex-German "Bismarck")

German s.s. "Schiller" homeward bound from New York wrecked at Scilly 8th May, 1875, with the loss of over 300 lives.

and New York there was no finer ship than the *Schiller,* due to arrive at Plymouth on Saturday. That vessel became a total wreck on Friday night, and with her were lost 310 of her passengers and crew. The *Schiller* was an iron steamer with seven water-tight compartments built on the Clyde by R. Napier in 1873, 380 feet in lenght, 40 ft. beam, and her gross tonnage 3,421. The wreck occurred on the Retarrier Ledges within three-quarters of a mile of the Bishop Rock. There is no doubt that the wreck is directly attributable to two causes -first, the dense fog which prevailed at the time, and secondly, the treacherous current which sets across the entrance to the Channel is a north-westerly direction. The 'Lady of the Isles' was at once despatched to the scene towing the Scilly lifeboat. She arrived too late. Point after point of the cruel jagged rocks forced themselves through the skin of the *Schiller* ripping open even that strong room wherein her mail bags were deposited, and nothing that had life was left, or could live, on board."

Reports published shortly after the sinking vary as to the exact number of passengers and crew who perished. Twenty-three mail bags were picked up after the wreck and divers later recovered something like £50,000 in specie and a considerable number of $20 pieces.

The German liner *Mosel* ran aground on the rocks below Lloyds Signal Station at the Lizard on 9th August, 1882, fortunately without loss of life. The 'Royal Cornwall Gazette' of 11th August, 1882, had this to say:-

"The largest mail steamer that, so far as is remembered, ever came ashore in the neighbourhood of the Lizard ran into the Point of the Beast about a mile to the east of the Lizard Lighthouse at 8 o'clock on Wednesday morning. The North German Lloyd steamer *Mosel* bound from Bremen via Southampton to New York with 600 passengers left Southampton at 4 o'clock on Tuesday afternoon and in running down the Channel in a thick fog by some means or other she got on the rocks immediately below the Lizard Signal Station. At the time she struck it is stated that the steamer was going at the rate of 13 knots an hour. The high rate of speed sent her three or four hundred yards on the flat ledge of rocks jutting out into the sea from the Point of the Beast where she remains with several degrees of list to port, and with her bottom very seriously damaged. The *Mosel* is about 3,200 tons burthen and is beautifully fitted up and provided with every accommodation. With but very few exceptions the whole of the passengers and crew were German. Several boats were quickly on the spot and no less than five tugs were there also in less than two hours after telegraphic communication to Falmouth from the Signal Station...... Some of the passengers were conveyed to Cadgwith and some to the Lizard, and eventually a large number were forwarded to Falmouth in steam tugs. The mails and specie were conveyed to Falmouth in the *Rosetta* steam tug owned by Deeble & Son......"

North German Lloyd liner "Mosel" ashore at the Lizard with tug
"Rosetta" alongside - August, 1882.

Steamer "Suffolk" ashore at The Lizard - September, 1886

From the issue of 18th August, 1882:-

"Heartless Conduct at the Lizard. At a Salvation Army meeting at Falmouth on Friday night a seamen's missionary who had been visiting the steerage passengers of the *Mosel*, domiciled in warehouses at Falmouth Docks, stated that much of the passengers' luggage had been pilfered at the Lizard while being transferred from the vessel. He saw one poor woman in great distress, her box having been robbed of 400 dollars. Several others had told him that their packages had been opened, valuables abstracted, and the boxes refilled with rubbish; and from other cases everything had been stolen except some books."

The response of the salvage people to these allegations is not known. Was there any truth in them? Was it likely that anybody travelling steerage would have 400 dollars in her luggage, particularly as the steamer was travelling TO, and not FROM, the United States? What the alleged 'valuables' were is not stated but steerage passengers were most unlikely to have any valuable possessions. Altogether not a very convincing story.

The *Mosel* became a total wreck.

Twenty-two years later, in June and July 1904, salvage operations were undertaken and several tons of sheet-iron, brass and spelter were recovered from the wreck. It had been reported that at the time the *Mosel* ran aground she had been carrying £2,000 worth of mercury in iron drums but there are no records as to whether or not it was ever recovered. The 'Royal Cornwall Gazette' of 14th July, 1904, merely said:-

"None of it has yet been salved."

Another victim of the cruel sea was the steamer *Suffolk* of London, 2,924 tons, which came to grief at Lizard Head on 28th September, 1886. There was no loss of life, the passengers and crew - 45 in all - being landed at Polpeor by the Lizard and Cadgwith Lifeboats. The "Royal Cornwall Gazette" of 8th October, 1886, said:-

"The steamship *Suffolk* which ran ashore on the rocks directly under Lizard Head on the afternoon of Tuesday last during dense fog when on a voyage from Baltimore to London, has entirely broken up and disappeared. Her cargo consisted of 161 bullocks on deck, 24,000 sacks of flour, about 500 casks of flour, 8,000 bushels of wheat, a large quantity of tabacco, resin, and provisions of all kinds, and has mostly washed out to sea. Nevertheless the coast for miles around is strewn with wreckage and cargo, together with a number of dead cattle which latter are now being buried with the utmost despatch. The first sale in connection with this steamer took place on Monday, 26 bullocks being sold by Mr. Pollard, the Auctioneer from Falmouth, at prices ranging from £9. 10s. to £17. 10s. Other cattle, alive but in places where there is no hope of getting them in safety to the top of the cliffs, will have to be slaughtered where they are. They have been kept alive by fodder and water lowered to them from the top of the cliffs. Great annoyance has been caused to the Lighthouse Authorities at the Lizard from the fact of some of the London papers having reported, in the account of the wreck, that the fog-horn was not blowing at the time of the disaster. Trinity House immediately telegraphed to their Superintendent there, at the same time sending down an official to inquire into the matter, and it is clearly proved that the fog-horn was not only blowing at the time but had set in motion as soon as the fog set in...... Hundreds of people visited the scene of the wreck and the coast on Sunday, the quiet little village having the appearance of a fair, the number of conveyances of all descriptions being very great."

On the 13th October, 1898, the new steamer *Mohegan* - 7,000 tons - of the Atlantic Transport Line, left Gravesend with 53 passengers, 96 crew, 6 cattlemen and a stowaway on board, under the command of Captain R. Griffiths, Commodore of the fleet, who at 2.30 p.m. on the 14th October signalled "All well" as he passed Prawle Point. Four and a half hours or so later, in fair weather, the *Mohegan* crashed on Vase Rock, one of the Manacles (maen eglos = church stones) and within twenty minutes all except portions of the masts and funnel were under water. The Porthoustock lifeboat was launched but a strong tide, and the fact that every light on the *Mohegan* went out when the engines stopped, hindered the work of rescue. The lifeboat did, however, succeed in rescuing 44 of the passengers and crew and the coxswain of the boat, James Hill, was later presented with a silver medal by the Royal National Lifeboat Institution for conspicuous service. Regarding this wreck the 'Royal Cornwall Gazette' of 30th October, 1898, said:

"On Friday evening in fairly clear weather an appalling disaster occurred off the Cornish coast. About 6 or 8 miles across the beautiful bay west of Falmouth Harbour lie the Manacle rocks. It was here on Friday evening that the liner *Mohegan* of the Atlantic Transport Company became a total wreck and caused the death of 97 lives. The *Mohegan* was a fine cargo and passenger steamship with a length of 500 feet and the indicated horse-power of her engines 5,000. She struck a ledge of rocks forming part of the dreaded Manacles. It was a clear night

Atlantic Transport Liner "Mohegan" wrecked on the
Manacles 13th Octr. 1898

U.S.M.S. "Paris" ashore at Lowland Point May, 1899

although the darkness was, according to all accounts, intense. There is nothing to explain how the vessel was so far out of her proper track, nor is there likely to be any adequate solution, as the officers, who alone could tell the tale, have perished.

Mr. A.S. Williams, agent for the Atlantic Transport Co., said on Saturday night: "It is absolutely impossible to account for the catastrophe. As it stands it is absolutely inexplicable."

A writer in the "Cornish Magazine" of December, 1898, under the heading "Why was the Mohegan lost?" asserted that the rocks along the Cornish coast from Penhallow to beyond the Lizard are more or less magnetic and thus affected the *Mohegan's* compass. This theory, however, has been pooh-poohed by many writers.

Seven months later, on 21st May, 1899, the American Liner *Paris* ran ashore at Lowland Point but fortunately without loss of life. Reports of this grounding filled several columns of the 'Royal Cornwall Gazette' of 25th May, 1899, and subsequent issues, of which the following are extracts:

"When early on Sunday morning it became noised abroad that the magnificent armoured liner *Paris* had gone on the Manacles, with a total complement of passengers and crew of 800 souls, there was a feeling of something near to consternation on all hands. The *Paris* left Southampton at noon on Saturday for New York with 380 passengers and 372 crew, Captain Watkins being in command. The weather was fine and the sea·smooth and a quick run was made to Cherbourg where about 50 passengers were embarked, mostly steerage, comprising French, German and Swiss peasants. Shortly after one o'clock on Sunday morning the officers were very much alarmed on hearing the look-out cry *"Land ahead."* The engines were immediately reversed but to no avail for the next instant after the alarm the huge vessel grated upon a hidden rock and came to a standstill on an even keel. The passengers hurried on deck and were met with comforting words and were assured of their safety. By the time dawn broke upon the scene of the disaster the passengers were relieved to find the beetling cliffs of the Cornish coast on one hand and the lifeboats of Coverack, Porthoustock and Falmouth within a short distance on the seaward side of the *Paris.* As the Falmouth tugs got alongside all the passengers were ordered to leave by the tug *Dragon* but, beyond the clothes they were dressed in, nothing was taken out of the vessel. The *Dragon* safely landed all the passengers at Falmouth shortly after 7 o'clock and they were taken charge of by the local agents of the American Line and well cared for in various hotels and at the Sailors' Home....... Salvage work was carried out with exceeding celerity. Early in the morning the *Mallard*, a boat belonging to the London Salvage Assocation, and tugs, were moored alongside the liner for the reception of as much of the general cargo as could be removed by the numerous derricks which were kept busily at work. To discover how the *Paris* came so far out of her proper course is as difficult a problem as in the case of the *Mohegan* but one is compelled to come to the conclusion that even apart from navigation the look-out was not as effective as it might have been."

From the issue of 1st June, 1899:
"Unsucessful efforts day by day to get the *Paris* afloat have now fully convinced those in authority of the real seriousness of the situation. Since the date of stranding a vast amount of mechanical force has been applied to the ship but all without avail."

From the issue of 15th June, 1899:
"*The Paris* has been on the Manacle reef for three weeks and her ultimate fate still hangs in the balance."

It was, in fact, not until several weeks later that the ship was refloated and the 'Royal Cornwall Gazette' of 20th July, 1899, was able to report:

"Midnight was at hand on Wednesday when the *Paris,* en route from the Manacles, came abreast of Pendennis Point, Falmouth. Connected by hawsers to the bow of the ship were the Falmouth tug *Victor* and the German salvage vessel *Sea Adler;* on the port side, where there was a marked list, stood a Dutch salvage vessel, the *E.M.Z. Svitzer;* on the starboard side a second German salvage boat, the *Berthide,* and astern the Falmouth tug *Dragon.*

From the issue of 17th August, 1899:
"The liner *Paris* left Falmouth for Milford Haven at about half-past eight on Monday morning. The vessel was unmoored and tow-ropes were attached to the salvage vessels *Berthide,* '*E.M.Z. Svitzer*' and *Sea Adler.* On getting into the bay the vessel's own engines were set in motion and the *Paris* proceeded slowly out of sight."

Whilst moored at Falmouth temporary repairs to the liner's damaged plates had been effected and eventually she was taken to the Belfast Shipyard of Harland & Wolff where she was cut in half, had one of her funnels removed, and a middle section of some twenty feet inserted amidships before being re-floated. The liner was then renamed *Philadelphia* and returned to the trans-Atlantic service plying between New York - Plymouth - Cherbourg - Southampton for many years. This was probably one of the most successful salvage operations ever undertaken.

During the time the *Paris* was fast on the rocks hundreds of sightseers had been taken by the *Queen of the Fal* and other pleasure steamers based at Falmouth, across the bay to view this great steamer and the salvage boats working to get her free. As a matter of interest it may be recorded that the Australian Cricket Team, then touring England under Joe Darling, were taken on such a trip by the *Queen of the Fal* on the conclusion of the two-day match they had played at Truro against an England XI captained by R.E. Foster. As the game resulted in a win for the Australians by 8 wickets no doubt they enjoyed the trip!

"Appalling Shipping Disaster. Over 600 lives lost." That was the heading of a news item in the 'Royal Cornwall Gazette' of 7th July, 1904, reporting the sinking on 28th June, 1904, of the Danish Liner *Norge* of the United Steamship Co., of Copenhagen, bound from Christiansund, Norway, to New York with well over 600 emigrant passengers and a crew of 64, after striking Helen's Reef, Rockall, a small uninhabited islet in the Atlantic some 290 miles off the west coast of Scotland.

As was to be the case of the *Titanic* eight years later the steamer had an insufficient number of life-boats to accommodate all her passengers and crew and there were only 128 survivors. The 'Royal Cornwall Gazette' report continues:

"The first lot of survivors were brought into Grimsby on Sunday by the steam trawler *Salvia.* Later news puts the loss of life at 637. Two more parties were landed at Tobermory on Monday bringing the total number of saved up to 128. The sailors on board the ill-fated vessel are stated to have behaved with great bravery and many stories of heroism are related."

Although not on the Atlantic run at the time, the large White Star Liner, *Suevic* of 12,500 tons, ran aground in thick fog on the Maenheere Reef off the Lizard on 17th November, 1907, en route to Southampton. The Lizard and the Cadgwith and the Porthleven lifeboats were launched in heavy seas and all 524 persons on board were saved. The R.N.L.I. awarded silver medals to the Revd. Harry Vyvyan, who piloted the Cadgwith lifeboat, to Edward Rutter, its coxwain, and to the coxwain and second coxwain - W.H. Mitchell and Edwin Mitchell - of the Lizard boat. The salvage vessels *Ranger* and regarded as a boon especially as with the prevailing rough wind the men are compelled to remain ashore and are paid the agreed rate notwithstanding."

Regarding the rescue of the cattle from this steamship some 147 boatmen of the Islands subsequently claimed compensation from the Atlantic Transport Company. That company made an offer of £600 which the men refused. In December, 1910, their claim came before the Admiralty Court and an Award of £780. 10s. was made in their favour.

The *Minnehaha* was torpedoed and sunk by a German submarine with the loss of 43 lives in 1917 shortly after the United States had entered the first World War on 6th April of that year.

The story of the sinking of the World's then most luxurious Liner, the White Star *Titanic* on her maiden voyage in April, 1912, is so well known and has been so expansively recorded in so many books that it is not necessary to enlarge upon it now. With something like fifteen water-tight compartments she was spoken of as "unsinkable." Carrying no less than 1,316 passengers and a crew of 892, on 14th April, 1912, she struck a huge iceberg and within a few hours slid beneath the waves carrying with her, 1,505 souls.

As was to be expected there were a number of Cornishmen and women on board this great steamer - sixty-nine in all, 58 as passengers and 11 of the crew. Of these, 18 passengers were saved (including Mrs. Ada West and her two daughters Constance and Barbara, of Truro) and 5 of the crew. Among the 40 Cornish passengers who were drowned were E.A. West (Ada West's husband) en route to Florida to start a fruit culture business, and Charles Fillbrook, a youth of 18 who had intended joining his uncle in Cleveland, also of Truro. Also among those drowned was the Chief Purser, Hugh McElroy, a brother of the Prior of Bodmin, Fr. Richard McElroy, C.R.L., who later became Parish Priest of Launceston. (See Addenda).

Memorial services were held at the Cathedral and in many Churches and Chapels throughout the county. The Mayor of Truro, Councillor W.G. Goodfellow, assisted by Miss Lily Paull of Trehaverne, opened a Relief Fund for the widows and orphans to which I see from the 'Royal Cornwall Gazette' of 2nd May, 1912, my parents contributed. Some £240 was thus raised in the City. Similar appeals were made in other towns and cities throughout the country and in all a considerable sum of money was distributed.

The Canadian Pacific *Empress of Ireland*, 15,646 tons, sailed from Quebec bound for Liverpool on 28th May, 1914, and that same night was in collision with the Norwegian s.s. *Storsdtad*. In a quarter of an hour, one of the quickest sinkings ever recorded, she was at the bottom of the sea with a loss of 1,106 lives.

Some six weeks before the outbreak of the first World War on 23rd June, 1914, to be exact - the Red Star Liner *Gothland* of 7,669 tons, struck the Zantman Rock in the Western Approaches off the Scillies in thick fog. The

Atlantic Transport liner "Minnehaha" ashore at Scilly -
April, 1910.

The ill-fated White Star Liner "Titanic" leaving on her first and
only voyage in April, 1912.

regarded as a boon especially as with the prevailing rough wind the men are compelled to remain ashore and are paid the agreed rate notwithstanding."

Regarding the rescue of the cattle from this steamship some 147 boatmen of the Islands subsequently claimed compensation from the Atlantic Transport Company. That company made an offer of £600 which the men refused. In December, 1910, their claim came before the Admiralty Court and an Award of £780. 10s. was made in their favour.

The *Minnehaha* was torpedoed and sunk by a German submarine with the loss of 43 lives in 1917 shortly after the United States had entered the first World War on 6th April of that year.

The story of the sinking of the World's then most luxurious Liner, the White Star *Titanic* on her maiden voyage in April, 1912, is so well known and has been so expansively recorded in so many books that it is not necessary to enlarge upon it now. With something like fifteen water-tight compartments she was spoken of as "unsinkable." Carrying no less than 1,316 passengers and a crew of 892, on 14th April, 1912, she struck a huge iceberg and within a few hours slid beneath the waves carrying with her, 1,505 souls.

As was to be expected there were a number of Cornishmen and women on board this great steamer - sixty-nine in all, 58 as passengers and 11 of the crew. Of these, 18 passengers were saved (including Mrs. Ada West and her two daughters Constance and Barbara, of Truro) and 5 of the crew. Among the 40 Cornish passengers who were drowned were E.A. West (Ada West's husband) en route to Florida to start a fruit culture business, and Charles Fillbrook, a youth of 18 who had intended joining his uncle in Cleveland, also of Truro. Also among those drowned was the Chief Purser, Hugh McElroy, a brother of the Prior of Bodmin, Fr. Richard McElroy, C.R.L., who later became Parish Priest of Launceston. (See Addenda).

Memorial services were held at the Cathedral and in many Churches and Chapels throughout the county. The Mayor of Truro, Councillor W.G. Goodfellow, assisted by Miss Lily Paull of Trehaverne, opened a Relief Fund for the widows and orphans to which I see from the 'Royal Cornwall Gazette' of 2nd May, 1912, my parents contributed. Some £240 was thus raised in the City. Similar appeals were made in other towns and cities throughout the country and in all a considerable sum of money was distributed.

The Canadian Pacific *Empress of Ireland,* 15,646 tons, sailed from Quebec bound for Liverpool on 28th May, 1914, and that same night was in collision with the Norwegian s.s. *Storsdtad.* In a quarter of an hour, one of the quickest sinkings ever recorded, she was at the bottom of the sea with a loss of 1,106 lives.

Some six weeks before the outbreak of the first World War on 23rd June, 1914, to be exact - the Red Star Liner *Gothland* of 7,669 tons, struck the Zantman Rock in the Western Approaches off the Scillies in thick fog. The

Atlantic Transport liner "Minnehaha" ashore at Scilly -
April, 1910.

The ill-fated White Star Liner "Titanic" leaving on her first and
only voyage in April, 1912.

s.s. GOTHLAND of the Atlantic Transport Line ashore in the
Western Approaches off the Scillies - June, 1914 - with salvage
boats alongside.

Liner "Samaria"
of 27,000 tons.

Gothland was homeward-bound - Montreal to Rotterdam - with 84
passengers and a crew of 170. By this date wireless telegraphy had been
installed on all Atlantic Liners and it was brought into use on this occasion.
The St. Mary's Lifeboat - *Henry Dundas* - and the St. Agnes Lifeboat - *Charles
Deere James* - were taken in tow by the steamer *Lyonesse* and proceeded to the
scene to take off the passengers and some of the crew. The sea being calm
there was no loss of life. The Captain and remaining members of the crew
stayed on board and after part of her cargo, grain and frozen meat, had been
jettisoned the *Gothland* was subsequently re-floated and, after undergoing
temporary repairs, was towed to Southampton. The interesting photograph
shows salvage work in progress.

AFTER THE FIRST WORLD WAR

It is not the purpose of this book to carry the story of the trans-Atlantic Liners beyond 1914 but it will be of some interest to make mention of some of the great luxurious leviathans which came into service after the conclusion of hostilities in November, 1918.

As a matter of fact by 1919 the proportions of the tonnage of ocean-going ships sailing under the flags of the various countries had undergone considerable changes from those mentioned on p.5. They then read: under the British flag 39%; under the U.S. flag 24%; under the Belgian flag 9%; under the Norwegian and Swedish flags 6%; under the Dutch flag 4%; under the Italian flag 4%; under the German flag considerably less than 1%; and under the French flag 6%.

It was 1922 before the Norddeutscher Lloyd line were able to resume sailings and 1928 before they were once again able to challenge the Cunarders. In 1929 the *Bremen* of 51,656 tons, and in 1930 the *Europa* of 49,746 tons, came down the slip-ways. In July, 1929, the *Bremen* made a record Atlantic west-bound crossing at a speed of 27.83 knots per hour, to be exceeded a year later when the *Europa* reached an average of 27.91 knots.

The Italians were not left in the cold and in 1932 from two Italian Shipyards came the *Rex* of 51,062 tons, and the *Conte di Savoia* of 48,502 tons. In 1933 the *Rex* took the blue-ribband with a westbound crossing at an average speed of 29.92 knots from Gibraltar to New York in 4 days 14 hours. Two years later the *Normandie* of the Compagnie Generale Trans-atlantique, 83,423 tons, fitted with turbo-electric engines and built by Chantiers et Ateliers at St. Nazaire, broke the record on her maiden voyage with an average speed of 30.99 knots. The *France* of this line, 66,348 tons, launched in 1962, is believed to be the longest passenger ship ever built, being 1,035 ft. in length.

The United States Lines, which came into existence in 1921, operated the ex-German Liners re-named:-

"George Washington"   ... ...   (ex-"Bremen")
"America"   ... ...   (ex-"Amerika")
"Leviathan"   ... ...   (ex-"Vaterland")

for some time after the end of the first World War, but the history of the United States Shipping Board was one of financial difficulties although the *America* continued on the Atlantic run until 1934.

For the old-established and most famous Cunard Line, with which the White Star Line had amalgamated in 1934, the year 1936 saw the arrival of the *Queen Mary*, 81,237 tons, which in August, 1938, made the east-bound crossing in 3 days, 20 hours, 42 minutes, at an average speed of 31.69 knots. A second Queen - the *Queen Elizabeth* of 83,673 tons, came into service in

Holland-Amerika Liner "STATENDAM" (1929 - the 3rd. of that name) 29,511 tons, entering the port of Rotterdam. The "Statendam" was destroyed by fire during the German invasion of the Netherlands in May, 1940.

Cunard "Aquitania" (centre) as a Hospital Ship and White Star "Olympic" (in rear) alongside Ocean Dock, Southampton, during the second World War.

Cunard R.M.S. QUEEN MARY - 81,237 tons.
Probably the most popular Atlantic Liner of all time.
(Photo: courtesy of R.W.R. Squier)

U.S. troops embarking in April, 1941, on board the U.S.S.
"Washington" which had been launched in 1938

The "UNITED STATES" - 53,329 tons - holder of the Blue Ribband for the fastest ever Atlantic crossing - 3 days, 10 hours, 40 minutes.

French s.s. "Normandie" 83,423 tons. (Stamp issued 23/4/1935 to commemorate maiden record breaking voyage.)

Cunard "Queen Elizabeth 2" at New York

A stateroom on board the "Queen Elizabeth 2"

February, 1940, and served as a troopship - as did the *Queen Mary* - until 1946 conveying more than a million and a half service men across the Atlantic.

If the interior fittings of the pre-1914 War steamships could be described as magnificent - particularly the first-class appointments - those on some of the Liners which crossed and re-crossed the Atlantic between the two Wars and subsequently can only be called sumptuous. As an example, on the French *Normandie*, previously mentioned, the huge Lounge and the smoking room were so constructed that they could, whenever desirable, become one enormous Grand Salon. The ship also provided a winter garden, a theatre, a spacious hall and what was called a Verandah-Grill on the deck below which was a great dining saloon said to be longer even than the Hall of Mirrors at Versailles. The ship's swimming-pool was constructed of marble and the Byzantine Chapel was the largest of any ship afloat.

Alas, this great ship's career came to an end when she was destroyed by fire whilst laid up at New York in 1942. She had been taken over by the U.S. Navy and was to have been re-named *Lafayette* but whilst conversion work was in progress the ship caught fire and sank and eventually had to be sold for scrap.

After the end of the second World War, the United Stages Congress, in 1950, voted a subsidy of $48,000,000 and a great super-liner named the *United States* was built by the Newport News Shipbuilding Company, with a length of 990 ft. a beam of 101 ft. and of 53,329 tons. On her maiden voyage this great ship reached the almost unbelievable average speed of 35.59 knots between the Ambrose Light and Bishop Rock, taking 3 days, 10 hours and 40 minutes in so doing. This remains the all-time record.

In 1957 the Duke of Windsor (formerly King Edward VIII) and the Duchess made one of their many crossings of the Atlantic as passengers on this ship. It has been said that they had been offered free passages by this steamer whenever they wanted them and consequently had ceased to travel by the Cunard Liners.

That even the great liners which operated the trans-Atlantic service in the post-war years - no longer, of course, burning coal but oil as fuel for their massive and powerful engines - were not free from disaster is evidenced by the sinking, in July, 1956, of the splendid Italian liner *Andrea Doria* of 29,000 tons, fitted with radar and every navigational aid. Nearing her port of destination - New York - the *Andrea Doria* was in collision with the Swedish liner *Stockholm* which struck the Italian ship on the starboard side killing some 43 persons. Fortunately the *Stockholm* and the *Ile de France,* which quickly answered the *Andrea Doria's* S.O.S. signals, were able to rescue the rest of the Italian liner's eleven hundred odd passengers and crew but the *Andrea Doria* sank the next day.

It has been said that the Cunarder *Queen Elizabeth 2* of 65,863 tons, launched in 1969, may be the last of the great super-liners to maintain a passenger service between Europe and America. In general the trans-Atlantic liners, like the clipper-ships of a previous century, are now but a memory of the great passenger steamships which sailed the seven seas. We shall never see their like again.

NOTES ON EMIGRATION FROM THE COUNTRIES OF EUROPE

During the half-century to 31st December, 1905, no less than 6,120,000 persons left the shores of Great Britain and Ireland to settle in the United States whilst during the sixteen years from 1890 to 1905, when emigration from Europe was probably at its height, 2,186,000 Germans and Austro-Hungarians; 931,000 Portuguese and Spaniards; over 900,000 Russians, Poles, and Lithuanians; and 627,000 Scandanavians, went overseas, the great majority to the United States. From Italy during the same period there were no less than 3,228,000 emigrants but a considerable number of these went to Brazil and Argentina.

Many of the European emigrants were Jews. For them "the United States" were words that signified a better life than anything their European ghettos could provide. During the first decade of this century a passage across the Atlantic from Hamburg to Boston or New York could be had for as little as ten dollars.

In fact overseas emigration from the countries of Europe continued at a high level until the outbreak of the first World War in August, 1914. In the six years immediately preceding that date 2,255,926 emigrants left Italy; 2,071,882 Great Britain and Ireland; 1,322,614 Austria-Hungary; 1,156,383 Spain and Portugal; 234,934 Scandanavian countries; 129,333 Germany, and 40,354 Belgium and the Netherlands. Those six years saw heavy emigration to Canada, Brazil, Argentina, Australia, New Zealand and South Africa but the United States continued to attract the greater number taking over 5,000,000 whilst the other countries mentioned absorbed slightly over 4,000,000.

In all cases of large scale immigration into a country there is, of course, some return movement. Many who have been successful return in order to end their lives in the old country. It is well known that many Italians who emigrated to the United States eventually returned to Italy and the same may be said, probably to a lesser degree, of British emigrants. Nevertheless the vast influx of immigrants and their assimilation into the life of the country undoubtedly contributed to the well-being and prosperity of the United States and helped in the framing of a constitution for people of many different views where they would have "a more abundant life" - (Roosevelt).

As a consequence of the restrictions on immigration into the United States shortly after the ending of the first World War, when the great flood of immigrants from the countries of Europe slowed to a trickle, many would-be emigrants sought new homes in other overseas countries and Great Britain in particular endeavoured to find outlets for her surplus population in the British Empire overseas. An Empire Settlement Act was passed in 1922 and in 1925 an Under-Secretaryship for Dominion affairs was constituted. Many thinly-populated expanses of the Empire thereafter attracted the bulk of emigration from Great Britain.

ADDENDA

White Star Liner *TITANIC* - Cornish people on board at the time of the disaster - April 1912.

PASSENGERS DROWNED

James Sleeman, Landrake.
Harry Cotterill, Penzance.
W.H. Nancarrow, Mount Charles.
Ernest Coon, Penwithick,
   St. Austell.
Charles Fillbrook, Truro.
Frederick Pengelly, Gunnislake.
H. Gale, Gunnislake.
S. Gale, Gunnislake.
Fred Giles, Porthleven.
Mr. and Mrs. J.H. Chapman,
   St. Neot.
Mr. and Mrs. Wm. Lobb, Bugle.
James Veale, Constantine.
Hayden Sobey, Porthallow.
Henry Rogers, Helston.
Mr. & Mrs. S. Old, Porthoustock.
Stephen Jenkin, St. Ives.
Joseph C. Nicholas, Penzance.
Richard Sliman, Fourlanes.

George Hocking, Penzance.
Percy Bailey, Penzance.
E.A. West, Truro.
W.H. Matthews, Penwithick,
   St. Austell.
Wm. Sanderson, St. Austell.
William Ware, Gunnislake.
George Green, Gunnislake.
F.J. Banfield, Helston.
Edgar Giles, Porthleven.
Mr. and Mrs A. Robins,
   Mount Charles.
Mrs. Lobb, Bodmin.
James Drew, Constantine.
Jago Smith, St. Keverne.
Wm. J. Berryman, St. Ives.
William Carbines, St. Ives.
William Gilbert, Breage.
Frank Andrew, Four Lanes.
Richard Otter, Fourlanes.

PASSENGERS SAVED

Miss Maud Sincock, St. Ives.
*John M. Davis, St. Ives.
Mrs. Emily Richards, Newlyn.
*William Richards, Newlyn.
*George Richards, Newlyn.
*Ralph Wells, Penzance.
Mrs. Ada West, Truro.
Miss Constance West, Truro.
Miss Barbara West, Truro.

Mrs. Agnes Davis, St. Ives.
Mrs. Eliza Hocking, Penzance.
Miss Nellie Hocking, Penzance.
Mrs. Addie Wells, Penzance.
Miss Joan Wells, Penzance.
Miss Susan Webber, Bude.
Miss Ellen Wilkes, Penzance.
Mrs. Lulu Drew, Constantine.
*Marshall Drew, Constantine.

* Children.

CREW DROWNED

H. Bristow, H. Creese, S. Ryler, F. Crouch, F. Pennal, E.T. Stone.

CREW SAVED

C.H. Pascoe, T. Blake, *R. Hitchens, A. Jewell, S. Rule.

(*Quartermaster Robert Hitchens of Penzance was at the wheel of the *Titanic* when she struck the iceberg and subsequently was in charge of one of the lifeboats which got away with survivors from the stricken vessel.)

For readers interested in details of great liners subsequent to the ending of the first World War, I recommend:-
    "The Atlantic Liners, 1925-1970."
by Frederick Emmons, published by David & Charles, Newton Abbot.

Europe to the U.S.A.
A typical full-rigged ship of the
19th century.